Changing
Materials

Chris Oxlade

 Cₗ   ᵢny

Crabtree Publishing Company

www.crabtreebooks.com

Editors: Hayley Leach, Adrianna Morganelli, Michael Hodge
Senior Design Manager: Rosamund Saunders
Designer: Ben Ruocco
Photographer: Philip Wilkins

Photo credits: Simon Belcher/Alamy p. 11, Manor Photography/Alamy p. 24, Niall McDiarmid/Alamy p. 20, Howard Sayer/Alamy p. 3, p. 10, Shout/Alamy p. 25, Lynne Siler Photography/Alamy p. 8, Janine Wiedel Photolibrary/Alamy p. 7, Ronnie Kaufman/Corbis p. 16, Peter Cade/Getty Images p. 22, Chris Everard/Getty Images p. 18, Jeri Gleiter/Getty Images p. 6, Marc Moritsch/National Geographic/Getty Images p. 13, Tim Thiel/Getty Images p. 15, Stephen Toner/Getty Images p. 14, Elizabeth Simpson/Getty Images p. 17, Japack/Photolibrary.com p. 9, Stefan Mokrzecki/ Photolibrary.com p. 23, John Zoiner/Photolibrary.com p. 12, Richard Hutching/Science Photo Library cover, p. 19, Philip Wilkins p. 21, pp. 26-27.

Activity & illustrations: Shakespeare Squared pp. 28-29.

Cover: A glass blower cuts molten glass.

Title page: Making a pear out of clay.

The publishers would like to thank the models Philippa and Sophie Campbell for appearing in the photographs.

Because of the nature of the Internet, it is possible that some website addresses (URLs) included in this book may have changed, or sites may have changed or closed down since publication. While the author and publisher regret any inconvenience this may cause the readers, no responsibility for any such changes can be accepted by either the author or the publisher.

Library and Archives Canada Cataloguing in Publication

Oxlade, Chris
      Changing materials / Chris Oxlade.

(Working with materials)
Includes index.
ISBN 978-0-7787-3638-7 (bound).--ISBN 978-0-7787-3648-6 (pbk.)

      1. Chemical reactions--Juvenile literature. 2. Chemical reactions--Experiments--Juvenile literature. 3. Change of state (Physics)--Juvenile literature. 4. Strength of materials--Juvenile literature. I. Title. II. Series: Oxlade, Chris. Working with materials.

QD501.O94 2007   j530.4'74   C2007-904320-8

Library of Congress Cataloging-in-Publication Data

Oxlade, Chris.
  Changing materials / Chris Oxlade.
        p. cm. -- (Working with materials)
  Includes index.
  ISBN-13: 978-0-7787-3638-7 (rlb)
  ISBN-10: 0-7787-3638-5 (rlb)
  ISBN-13: 978-0-7787-3648-6 (pb)
  ISBN-10: 0-7787-3648-2 (pb)
  1. Chemical reactions--Juvenile literature. 2. Chemical reactions--Experiments--Juvenile literature. 3. Change of state (Physics)--Juvenile literature. 4. Strength of materials--Juvenile literature. I. Title. II. Series.

  QD501.O9185 2008
  530.4'74--dc22   2007027419

Crabtree Publishing Company

www.crabtreebooks.com   1-800-387-7650

**Published in Canada
Crabtree Publishing**
616 Welland Ave.
St. Catharines, Ontario
L2M 5V6

**Published in the United States
Crabtree Publishing**
PMB16A
350 Fifth Ave., Suite 3308
New York, NY 10118

Published by CRABTREE PUBLISHING COMPANY
Copyright © **2008**

CONTENTS

Words in **bold** can be found in the glossary on page 30

Changing materials

Everything around you is made
up of materials. Everyday materials
include wood, plastic, metal, and
fabrics. Materials change all around
you every day. Ice turns to water
in drinks, and wood burns on bonfires.

↓ *Snow and ice*
change to water
when they warm up.

Imagine cookies baking, a candle burning, and ice melting. These materials are changing. The cookies are turning hard, the candle wax is being used up, and the ice is turning to water.

↑ *These pots were heated in a **kiln**. The soft clay has turned hard.*

Changing shape

A solid material is a material that stays in the same shape. Wood and plastic are solid materials. We can change the shape of solid materials by pulling and pushing on them. We can squash, stretch, bend, or twist these materials.

↓ *Each bow is made of solid plastic. They bend when the archers pull the bowstrings.*

8

← *Water is a liquid. It takes the shape of the container that it goes into.*

A liquid is a material that changes shape by itself. If you put liquid into a container, the liquid flows and fills up the bottom of the container.

9

Bending and breaking

When you stretch, squash, bend, or twist materials, such as modeling clay or bread dough, they stay in their new shapes. Some materials return to their original shapes. For example, an elastic band springs back into shape when you stop pulling it.

← *It is easy to make new shapes with modeling clay.*

↑ *Chocolate hardly bends at all before it snaps. We say that it is a **brittle** material.*

It's a fact!

A spring is a coil of strong wire. It springs back into shape after it is squashed or stretched. Cars and pens have springs inside them.

Some materials are easier to squash, stretch, bend, and twist than others are. Rubber is easy to bend, wood is harder to bend, and metal is very difficult to bend. Some materials can break if we try to change their shape too much.

11

Melting materials

Ice is a solid material, and water is a liquid. When a material changes from a solid to a liquid, we say that it melts. Melting happens when a solid material gets warmer. Ice cubes melt because they warm up outside the freezer.

← Metals are melted so that they can be made into new shapes in **molds**.

← *When **molten lava** from a volcano cools, it turns to solid rock.*

The reverse of melting is called "freezing" or "solidifying". This is when a liquid turns into a solid. Freezing happens when a liquid material is cooled. When you put water in a freezer, the water cools. This makes it freeze and turn into ice.

13

Boiling materials

When water is heated in a pan, the water gets hotter and hotter. Bubbles of gas rise from the bottom of the pan. Some of the water is changing into gas. This change is called "boiling". The gas is called "water vapor" or "steam".

↓ Boiling mud pools are created when water turns to steam deep underground. The steam bubbles up through the mud.

← *Water vapor is hitting this pot lid as the water boils. The water vapor cools quickly and turns back to water.*

A gas can turn into liquid, too. This change is called **"condensation"**. Boiling water in a pot turns into water vapor. The vapor cools above the pot. It turns back into tiny water droplets.

Water vapor in the air

After it rains, the ground is wet, and puddles form. If the sun's heat dries the ground, the puddles disappear. This is because water turns into water vapor and mixes with the air. This change is called **"evaporation"**.

↓ These paints are runny because they contain water. The paint dries when the water evaporates.

16

↑ *Clouds are made of tiny droplets of water. The drops are made when water vapor in the air cools.*

There is always some water vapor in the air. When the air cools, some of the water vapor turns back into liquid water, which forms clouds. On a hot day, the air around a can of cold drink cools, and small drops of water appear on the can.

Hard and soft

When ice melts, it changes from solid ice to liquid water. When some materials are heated, they get softer and softer before turning into liquids. Chocolate and butter turn soft in a warm room.

↓ *This butter has become soft enough to spread.*

18

↑ *Glass turns soft when it is very hot.*

Materials that turn soft when they are heated are easy to make into shapes. A chocolate bar is made by pouring hot, **runny** chocolate into a mold. When the chocolate cools, it turns hard, making a solid bar.

It's a fact!

Plastic objects, such as plastic drink bottles, are made in molds. Hot, runny plastic is put into a mold. Then the mold is cooled, making the plastic turn hard.

19

Dissolving materials

Salt is often added to water for cooking vegetables. The grains of salt gradually break up into pieces that are too small to see. When a material breaks up in water like this, we say that it **dissolves**. The mixture of the salt and water is called a **"solution"**.

← *When you stir sugar into a drink, the sugar dissolves in the liquid.*

← *These crystals of salt formed when a solution of water and salt dried up.*

We can get the dissolved material out of a solution by removing the water. If we leave a dish of solution in a warm place, the water gradually evaporates (see page 16). When all of the water has gone, the material is left in the dish.

It's a fact!

We cannot clean oily paints from brushes with water. Instead, we use a liquid called turpentine. Oil dissolves in turpentine but not in water.

Changing forever

Changes such as squashing and melting can be **reversed**. An elastic band can return to its original shape, and water can be frozen to make ice again. Some changes cannot be reversed. For example, when an egg is cooked, it changes forever.

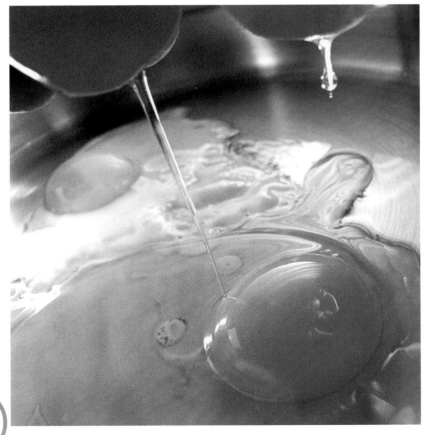

← Heating an egg makes the egg turn solid. This change can never be reversed.

← Material changes happen naturally, too. These leaves gradually change as they rot away.

It's a fact!

When cement, water, sand, and gravel are mixed together, they change into a new material called "concrete".

When you bake a cake, a permanent change happens. The ingredients in the cake mixture, such as sugar and flour, are changed into new materials that make up the baked cake.

Burning materials

When a candle burns, the wax in the candle changes forever. As it changes, it makes heat and light that come from the flame. Burning is a useful way to change materials. We use it to make heat for cooking and for keeping warm.

↓ *Wood burns on a fire. The wood is turned into ash.*

↑ *Foam stops oxygen from getting to the burning material, so the fire goes out.*

Burning cannot happen without **oxygen** in the air. Firefighters often put out a fire by covering the burning material. They cover it with **foamy** water.

It's a fact!

A fuel is a material that we burn to make heat. Gas, coal, and wood are all fuels.

25

See for yourself!

Making salt crystals

Try this experiment to see how evaporation works.

What you need	
glass bowl	table salt
plastic saucer	teaspoon

① Put 1 cup (250 mL) of warm (not hot) water in the glass bowl.

② Add a teaspoon of table salt. Stir until the salt dissolves.

③ Keep adding teaspoons of salt one at a time and stir. Stop adding salt when you cannot make it dissolve.

④ Pour a little of the salt solution onto a plastic saucer and leave the saucer in a warm place.

⑤ Look at the saucer every hour, and write down what you see. How much of the water has gone? Can you see any salt? After a few hours, all of the water will be gone. It has evaporated. The salt from the solution is left on the saucer.

26

Making plastic

Find out how you can make plastic using everyday materials.

What you need

non-skimmed milk	coffee filter
vinegar	dessert spoon
plastic dish	

① Put four dessert spoons of milk into a plastic bowl.

② Add one dessert spoon of vinegar. Stir the milk and vinegar together.

③ Pour the mixture into a coffee filter. Leave the filter over the bowl for about 15 minutes. Clear liquid will ooze out of the filter.

④ The white solid left in the filter is a type of plastic. It was made when the vinegar and milk changed when they were mixed together.

⑤ Leave the filter in a warm place. When the plastic dries, it will feel hard.

③

④

Weather in a bag

Watching condensation and evaporation at work

On a sunny day, try this experiment to see water change states.

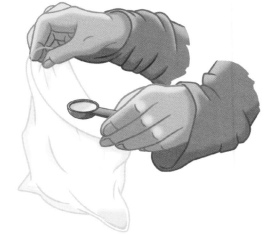

What you need

clear plastic bag

teaspoon

water

pencil

twist tie

masking tape

paper

1. Pour two teaspoons of water into a clear plastic bag.

2. Blow enough air inside the bag to fill it completely. Quickly seal the bag with a twist tie. The bag should look like a balloon.

3. Find a window that receives good sun exposure. Tape the bag to the window.

4. Every hour, check the bag. What do you notice? Is the water still present? If so, in what form? Write down your observations on a sheet of paper.

What you will see:

Over several hours, the water placed in the bag will slowly evaporate. As this happens, the water vapor will then condense to form tiny water droplets on the side of the bag. Also, there will appear to be a slight fog in the bag. This is water vapor that has condensed and formed a cloud. You have just created your own weather in a bag!

Glossary

brittle Something that snaps easily

condensation When a gas turns into a liquid

dissolve To break up into tiny pieces in a liquid

evaporate When a liquid changes into a gas

foam A material made up of many bubbles that are joined to each other

kiln A large oven used for making clay hard

lava Hot, molten rock from a volcano

molten When something is heated until it melts

mold A block of material with a space inside. When molten material is poured into a mold, it forms an object the shape of the space

oxygen A gas that is in the air

runny When something flows like a liquid

reversed When something is changed back into what it was before

solution A liquid with another material dissolved in it

Further information

BOOKS

How We Use: Metals/Paper/Rubber/Wood
by Chris Oxlade, Raintree (2005)

A Material World: It's Glass/It's Metal/It's Plastic/It's Wood
by Kay Davies and Wendy Oldfield, Wayland (2006)

Investigating Science: How do we use materials?
by Jacqui Bailey, Franklin Watts (2005)

WEBSITES

www.bbc.co.uk/schools/revisewise/science/materials/09_act.shtml
Animated examples and quiz about changing materials

www.strangematterexhibit.com
Fun site about the properties of materials

PLACES TO VISIT

American Museum of Science and Energy, Tennessee
www.amse.org

The Children's Museum of Science and Technology, New York
www.cmost.com

The Discovery Center for Science and Technology, California
www.discoverycntr.org

Index

Printed in the USA